The Sports Wiz Trivia Quiz

by Steve Heldt

RED-LETTER PRESS, INC.

THE SPORTS WIZ TRIVIA QUIZ
Copyright ©2001 Red-Letter Press, Inc.
ISBN: 0-940462-50-8
All Rights Reserved
Printed in the United States of America

For information address:

Red-Letter Press, Inc.
P.O. Box 393, Saddle River, NJ 07458

ACKNOWLEDGMENTS

Cover design
and typography: s.w.artz, inc.

Editorial: Ellen Fischbein

Contributors: Angela Demers
Jack Kreismer
Mike Ryan

INTRODUCTION

Red-Letter Press proudly steps up to the plate with *The Sports Wiz Trivia Quiz*. Formatted in ten-question quizzes, it features an all-star selection of stumpers from the world of sports.

Steve Heldt brings you a book loaded with trivia ... Who was the first player in baseball history to have his number retired? ... What's the width of a football field? ... Name the only boxer to fight Rocky Marciano and Muhammad Ali.

The answers are all inside so now find out if you're a sports wiz or wannabe.

Jack Kreismer
Publisher

FIRST OF ALL

Can you name ...

1. The first winner of the Kentucky Derby?

2. The first pro athlete to appear on the front of a Wheaties box?

3. The first woman to qualify for the Indianapolis 500?

4. The first NHL expansion team to win the Stanley Cup?

5. The first golfer to win a sudden-death playoff at The Masters?

6. The first gymnast to attain a perfect score of 10 in the Olympics?

7. The first shot-putter to crack the 70-foot barrier?

8. The first college basketball player to win the Sullivan Award as the nation's top amateur athlete?

9. The first tight end elected to the Pro Football Hall of Fame?

10. The first NBA player to win back-to-back MVP Awards?

Sec.	Row	Seat	
82	E	17	Enter Gate B

"I am a professional tennis player. I have a friend who is a nun and her social life is better than mine."

–Wendy Turnbull

ANSWERS

1. Aristedes, 1875

2. Pete Rose, 1985

3. Janet Guthrie, 1977

4. The Philadelphia Flyers won it in 1974.

5. Fuzzy Zoeller defeated Tom Watson and Ed Sneed in 1979.

6. Romanian Nadia Comaneci did it in 1976 at the age of 14.

7. Randy Matson reached 70 feet, 7 inches in 1964.

8. Princeton's Bill Bradley, 1965

9. Mike Ditka, 1988

10. The Knicks' Willis Reed won it in 1972 and '73.

FULL SEASON

Sec. 17
Row K
Seat 22
Gate F

"A race track is where windows clean people."

–Comedian Danny Thomas

GRAB BAG

1. Quick! Who invented basketball?

2. What animal is the mascot for the football team at West Point?

3. This player blazed a trail when he was called for a record 38 technical fouls in the 1999-2000 NBA season. Who was he?

4. These two teams battled for seven hours in a 2000 NHL playoff game. Name them.

5. Two players have won baseball's Triple Crown twice. One was Ted Williams. Who was the other?

6. On what three continents did Muhammad Ali win his four heavyweight titles?

7. The 2000 Indianapolis 500 was the first with two female drivers. One was Lyn St. James. Who was the other?

8. How many gold medal winners were from the United States at the 1980 Summer Olympics?

9. Name the first golfer to earn two million dollars in a season.

10. Who is the only female owner of an NFL team?

ANSWERS

1. James Naismith
2. A mule
3. Rasheed Wallace, Portland
4. The Philadelphia Flyers and Pittsburgh Penguins
5. Rogers Hornsby, 1922 and '25
6. North America, Asia and Africa
7. Sarah Fisher — Neither driver finished the race.
8. None — This country boycotted the Olympics that year.
9. Tiger Woods, 1997
10. Georgia Frontiere, St. Louis Rams

"He's a terrific guy and the world's quietest person. The night he broke (Lou) Gehrig's record, he went out and painted the town beige."

–Billy Ripken, about brother Cal

Sec. 16

Row 51

Seat 7a

Enter Gate G

Lower Tier

WHO AM I?

1. I became the first boxer to regain the heavyweight title when I knocked out Ingemar Johansson in 1960.

2. I'm the only man in the Baseball Hall of Fame whose last name begins with the letter "I".

3. I was the first American to win the NHL Conn Smythe Trophy as playoff MVP in 1994.

4. They used me for the model in the official NBA logo. I'm the silhouetted player you see on all NBA uniforms.

5. I succeeded the legendary Adolph Rupp as basketball coach at the University of Kentucky.

6. I became the first NHL player to score more than 100 points in a season when I tallied 126 in the 1968-69 season.

7. I was the first foreign-born golfer to win The Masters.

8. I am the only man to play for the Braves in Boston, Milwaukee and Atlanta.

9. I'm the only American male tennis player to win three straight U.S. Opens.

10. Before my broadcasting career, I earned Super Bowl rings with three different teams.

ANSWERS

1. Floyd Patterson

2. Monte Irvin

3. Brian Leetch, New York Rangers

4. Jerry West

5. Joe B. Hall

6. Phil Esposito, Boston Bruins

7. South African Gary Player, 1961

8. Hall of Fame third baseman Eddie Matthews

9. Pete Sampras

10. Matt Millen, with the Raiders, 49ers and Redskins

Sec.	Row	Seat
82	E	17

Enter Gate B

"Wasn't watching."

> *–Broadcaster Phil Rizzuto, when asked what "ww" stood for in his score book following an at-bat*

FIRST IN LINE

Can you name ...

1. The first college football player to win the Heisman Trophy twice?

2. The first NBA player to score 20,000 points in his career?

3. The first golfer to win the U.S. Open and the British Open in the same year?

4. The first wild card team to win a Super Bowl?

5. The first female athlete to appear on the front of a Wheaties box?

6. The first NHL player to score 50 goals in a season?

7. The first pitcher to throw a complete game, 1-0 shutout in the seventh game of a World Series?

8. The first woman tennis player to win nine singles titles at Wimbledon?

9. The first announcers on ABC's *Monday Night Football*?

10. The first jockey to win the Kentucky Derby five times?

ANSWERS

1. Archie Griffin, Ohio State, 1974 and '75

2. Bob Pettit, St. Louis Hawks

3. Bobby Jones, 1926

4. The Oakland Raiders beat Philadelphia, 27-10, in Super Bowl XV.

5. Olympic gold medal gymnast Mary Lou Retton

6. Maurice Richard of Montreal, in the 1944-45 season

7. The Yankees' Ralph Terry, who blanked the Giants, 1-0, in the 1962 series

8. Martina Navratilova, 1978, 1979, 1982-87 and 1990

9. Keith Jackson, Howard Cosell and Don Meredith

10. Eddie Arcaro

Sec. 07

Row 19

Seat 12

Enter
Gate C
Upper Tier

**"I never cease to amaze myself.
I say this humbly."**

-Boxing promoter Don King

FULL SEASON TICKET

PIGSKIN POTPOURRI

1. Name the two TV networks that broadcast the first Super Bowl.

2. What stadium hosts the Sugar Bowl?

3. Who is the only NFL player to rush for 100 yards in eleven straight games?

4. Which Super Bowl was the first played on artificial turf?

5. What NFL team was named for its owner/coach?

6. How many officials work a pro football game?

7. Name the first coach of the Baltimore Ravens.

8. He owns the all-time career mark for catches and receiving yardage for the Dallas Cowboys. Who is he?

9. True or false? Three NFL teams play their home games in New York State.

10. Who coined the term "The Super Bowl"?

ANSWERS

1. NBC and CBS

2. The Superdome in New Orleans

3. Marcus Allen

4. Super Bowl V

5. The Cleveland Browns, for Paul Brown

6. Seven — the referee, umpire, head linesman, line judge, back judge, side judge and field judge

7. Brian Billick

8. Michael Irvin

9. False — Only the Bills play in New York. The Giants and Jets play in East Rutherford, NJ.

10. Kansas City Chiefs owner Lamar Hunt

"They thought lacrosse was what you would find in la church."

–Robin Williams

| Sec. 16 |
| Row 51 |
| Seat 7a |
| Enter Gate G |
| Lower Tier |

YOU WERE THERE

On March 2, 1962 Wilt Chamberlain scored 100 points against the New York Knicks. How much do you know about the game?

1. What was the final score of the game?

2. Name the city where the game was played.

3. Whose NBA scoring record was broken by Chamberlain's performance?

4. True or false? Wilt missed only four free throws in the game.

5. Who was the second leading scorer for the Warriors that night?

6. What team record, since broken, was set by the Knicks?

7. Chamberlain set five individual records during the game. One was most field goals. How many did he make?

8. True or false? Fewer than five thousand people were eyewitnesses to the record-setting feat.

9. Three Knicks scored over thirty points in the game. Cleveland Buckner (33) and Willie Naulls (31) were two of them. Who was the third?

10. The center guarding Wilt fouled out after scoring seven points. Later in his career, he was one of three players traded for Chamberlain. Name him.

ANSWERS

1. Warriors — 169, Knickerbockers — 147
2. Hershey, PA
3. His own — Wilt scored 78 points against the Lakers in 1961.
4. True
5. Al Attles scored 17 points.
6. Their 147 points was the most ever scored by a losing team.
7. Thirty-six
8. True — Attendance was 4,124 people.
9. Richie Guerin led the team with 39 points.
10. Darrall Imhoff

"Managing is getting paid for home runs someone else hits."

–Casey Stengel

| Sec. 16 |
| Row 51 |
| Seat 7a |
| **Enter Gate G** Lower Tier |

ONE AND ONLY

1. Name the only undefeated NFL team to win a Super Bowl.

2. Only one NHL team has won five consecutive Stanley Cups. Which one?

3. Who are the only two pitchers to have thrown no-hitters in both the American and National Leagues?

4. Name the only American golfer to have won five British Opens.

5. He's the only New York Knick to win a scoring title in the NBA. Name him.

6. Winning one tennis Grand Slam is tough. He's the only one to win two. Who is he?

7. Who is the only Heisman Trophy winner to play on a college team with a losing record?

8. Name the only horse to beat the legendary Man O' War.

9. This southpaw threw a no-hitter in four consecutive seasons, the only major-leaguer to do so. What's his name?

10. Packers' coach Vince Lombardi lost only one NFL post-season game in his career. What team beat him?

ANSWERS

1. The 1972 Miami Dolphins

2. The Montreal Canadians, 1955-56 through 1959-60

3. Jim Bunning and Nolan Ryan

4. Tom Watson

5. Bernard King, in the 1984-85 season

6. Rod Laver, 1962 and 1969

7. Paul Hornung played on the 1956 Notre Dame team that went 2-8.

8. Upset, in an upset, in 1919

9. Sandy Koufax, Dodgers, from 1962-65

10. The Philadelphia Eagles, 17-13, in the 1960 NFL championship game

---

"He'll scream from the 60th row of bleachers that you missed a marginal call in the center of the interior line and then won't be able to find his car in the parking lot."

–NFL referee Jim Tunney, on some fans

Sec. 16

Row 51

Seat 7a

**Enter
Gate G**
Lower Tier

GRAB BAG

1. Name the former Oakland Raider who played Apollo Creed in the Rocky films.

2. After Red Auerbach, the next four Boston coaches were former Celtics. How many can you name?

3. In what state is horse racing's The Preakness held?

4. Has tennis player Pete Sampras ever won his sport's French Open?

5. What are racing great A.J. Foyt's first two names?

6. True or false? The Dallas Cowboys were the first NFL team to display numbers on the sides of their uniform pants.

7. Who set the record for rookies when he hit 49 home runs in 1987?

8. Quick! Name the opposing head coaches in the first Super Bowl.

9. The Boston Red Sox won one World Series in the 1900s. What year was it?

10. What horse won racing's first Triple Crown?

ANSWERS

1. Carl Weathers
2. Bill Russell, Tom Heinsohn, Tom Sanders and Dave Cowens
3. Maryland
4. No
5. Anthony Joseph
6. True
7. Mark McGwire, Oakland A's
8. Vince Lombardi — Packers; Hank Stram — Chiefs
9. 1918
10. Sir Barton, 1919

Sec.	Row	Seat
82	E	17

Enter Gate B

"He slides into second with a stand-up double."

-San Diego Padres broadcaster Jerry Coleman

IF YOU BUILD IT ...

Name the major league teams that call these ballparks "home."

1. Coors Field
2. Comiskey Park
3. The Ballpark in Arlington
4. Camden Yards
5. Turner Field
6. Jacobs Field
7. Pacific Bell Park
8. Safeco Field
9. Comerica Park
10. Enron Field

FULL SEASON

Sec. 17
Row K
Seat 22
Gate F

"Dealing with the press. After the demands of a game, my mind needs a rest."

-Indiana basketball coach Bobby Knight, when asked about the part of coaching he likes best

ANSWERS

1. Colorado Rockies
2. Chicago White Sox
3. Texas Rangers
4. Baltimore Orioles
5. Atlanta Braves
6. Cleveland Indiana
7. San Francisco Giants
8. Seattle Mariners
9. Detroit Tigers
10. Houston Astros

Sec. 07

Row 19

Seat 12

Enter
Gate C
Upper Tier

**"My wife made me a millionaire.
I used to have three million."**

–Hockey Hall of Famer Bobby Hull

FULL SEASON TICKET

BY THE NUMBERS

Do you know …

1. The number of times Jack Nicklaus has won The Masters?

2. The number of career home runs hit by Willie Mays in the World Series?

3. The width, in feet, of a hockey rink?

4. The number of French Open titles won by tennis player Chris Evert?

5. The number worn by every winning Super Bowl quarterback from 1972 to 1980?

6. The number of post-season appearances by Reggie Jackson, a major league record?

7. Ken Griffey Jr.'s uniform number?

8. The minimum age of a golfer to play on the PGA Senior Tour?

9. The number of teams in the NBA?

10. The number of games in which Nolan Ryan had ten or more strikeouts?

ANSWERS

1. 6
2. 0
3. 85
4. 7
5. 12
6. 77
7. 30
8. 50
9. 29
10. 215

"I'm a four-wheel-drive-pickup type of guy, and so is my wife."

–Boston Red Sox outfielder Mike Greenwell

Sec. 16

Row 51

Seat 7a

Enter Gate G

Lower Tier

ALMA MATER

Match the athlete with the school he attended.

1. Dan Marino
2. John McEnroe
3. Barry Bonds
4. Karl Malone
5. Anthony Munoz
6. David Duval
7. Roger Clemens
8. Anfernee Hardaway
9. Sterling Sharpe
10. Glen Rice

A. Texas
B. South Carolina
C. Michigan
D. USC
E. Arizona State
F. Stanford
G. Georgia Tech
H. Pittsburgh
I. Louisiana Tech
J. Memphis State

Sec. 82   Row E   Seat 17   Enter Gate B

"Well, if it's undisputed what's all the fighting about?"

–George Carlin, on the heavyweight boxing title

ANSWERS

1. H
2. F
3. E
4. I
5. D
6. G
7. A
8. J
9. B
10. C

FULL SEASON

Sec. 17
Row K
Seat 22
Gate F

"They wanted an arm and a leg."

–Tennis great Martina Navratilova, on why she never insured her left arm with Lloyds of London

DEPARTMENT OF WEIGHTS AND MEASURES

Do you know ...

1. The distance from the basket to the three-point line in the NBA?

2. The diameter of a golf hole?

3. The size of the bases, excluding home plate, in baseball?

4. The length of Mike Powell's record long jump in 1991?

5. The width of a football field, in feet?

6. The thickness of a hockey puck?

7. The maximum allowable weight of a golf ball?

8. The official distance of a marathon?

9. The distance from the pitcher's rubber to home plate in Major League Baseball?

10. The height of the roof of America's first domed stadium, the Astrodome?

ANSWERS

1. 23 feet, 9 inches
2. 4.25 inches
3. 15 inches X 15 inches
4. 29 feet, 4 1/2 inches
5. 160 feet
6. 1 inch
7. 1.62 ounces
8. 26 miles, 385 yards
9. 60 feet, 6 inches
10. 208 feet, equivalent to an eighteen-story building

Sec. 07

Row 19

Seat 12

Enter
Gate C
Upper Tier

"He hit a pop-up against us one day that
went so high, all nine guys on our team
called for it."

*–Florida Marlins coach Rich Donnelly, on the
super strength of Mark McGwire*

FULL SEASON TICKET

GRAB BAG

1. Who was the first NHL goalie to score a goal?

2. In 1983, the United States lost the America's Cup for the first time in 132 years. What nation's yacht beat them?

3. How many points does a team get for a safety in the NFL?

4. True or false? Richie Ashburn won more National League batting titles than Willie Mays.

5. Who is the winningest head coach in NBA history?

6. Coaching legends Tom Landry and Vince Lombardi worked together for four years as assistant coaches for what team?

7. Who took over for Woody Hayes as football coach at Ohio State?

8. What is a stimpmeter?

9. Who holds the record for most overtime playoff goals in the NHL?

10. How many interceptions did Joe Montana throw in his Super Bowl career?

ANSWERS

1. Ron Hextall, Philadelphia, 1987
2. Australia
3. Two
4. True — Ashburn won in 1955 and 1958. Mays won his only title in 1954.
5. Lenny Wilkens
6. New York Giants, 1954-58
7. Earle Bruce
8. It's used in golf to measure the speed of the greens on a golf course.
9. Maurice Richard, Montreal
10. None

Sec. 82
Row E
Seat 17
Enter Gate B

"I quit school in the fifth grade because of pneumonia. Not because I had it but because I couldn't spell it."

–Fighter Rocky Graziano

OH, BROTHER!

Ten sets of brothers have homered in a game in major league history. Match the family names with the first names.

1.	Boone	A.	Hank and Tommie
2.	Giambi	B.	Rick and Wes
3.	Aaron	C.	Jason and Jeremy
4.	Waner	D.	Al and Tony
5.	Alou	E.	Cal and Billy
6.	Conigliaro	F.	Aaron and Bret
7.	Farrell	G.	Paul and Lloyd
8.	Cuccinello	H.	Graig and Jim
9.	Nettles	I.	Billy and Tony
10.	Ripken	J.	Matty and Jesus

FULL SEASON
Sec. 17
Row K
Seat 22
Gate F

"I prefer fast food."

–San Francisco Giants coach Rocky Bridges, on why he won't eat snails

ANSWERS

1. F
2. C
3. A
4. G
5. J
6. I
7. B
8. D
9. H
10. E

"They've (the Baseball Hall of Fame) got a broadcasters' wing and a players' wing. Maybe one day they'll have a chicken wing." *–Ted Giannoulas, a.k.a. the "Chicken"*	**Sec. 16** **Row 51** **Seat 7a** **Enter Gate G** Lower Tier

FEELING A DRAFT

1. True or false? QB John Elway was the 1983 number one pick of the Baltimore Colts.

2. The Tampa Bay Buccaneers' first-ever draft choice was a defensive lineman who was elected to the Pro Football Hall of Fame in 1995. Who was he?

3. In 1979, the Lakers had two first-round choices in the NBA draft. With one, they took Magic Johnson. Whom did they select with the other pick?

4. True or false? Cy Young Award winner Tom Glavine was a 1984 fourth-round draft pick of the NHL's Los Angeles Kings.

5. This defensive lineman from TCU, who went on to play in eleven pro bowls, was the first draft pick in the history of the Dallas Cowboys. Name him.

6. Of all the players selected number one in the NBA draft in the '70s, only one won the Rookie of the Year Award. Who was he?

7. In 1965, the Chicago Bears selected a running back and a linebacker with their first-round picks. Hall of Famers, they are both considered to be one of the best to play their positions. Who are they?

8. Quick! Name the Heisman Trophy winner who was also an NBA first-round choice in 1994.

9. Who was the first draft pick, ever, for the NBA's Vancouver Grizzlies?

10. Name the Portland general manager who selected Sam Bowie instead of Michael Jordan in the 1984 NBA draft.

ANSWERS

1. True — The Colts later traded him to Denver.
2. Lee Roy Selmon
3. Brad Holland, a guard from UCLA
4. True
5. Bob Lilly
6. Kareem Abdul-Jabbar, Milwaukee Bucks, 1970
7. Running back Gale Sayers and linebacker Dick Butkus
8. Charlie Ward, New York Knicks
9. Bryant Reeves, Oklahoma State, 1995
10. Jack Ramsay

"On the day of the race, a lot of people want you to sign something just before you get in the car so that they can say they got your last autograph."

-A.J. Foyt

Sec. 16

Row 51

Seat 7a

Enter Gate G
Lower Tier

GRAB BAG

1. Who are the only two brothers enshrined in the Baseball Hall of Fame?

2. Who won the NBA scoring title for the 1999-2000 season?

3. This Montreal Canadien introduced the goalie mask in 1959. Name him.

4. Over which eye does the warrior wear a patch on the Oakland Raiders helmet?

5. Who was the jockey that rode Affirmed to horse racing's Triple Crown in 1978?

6. Which team won the 1992 NFC Championship without scoring a touchdown?

7. Name the two players who made up the Houston Rockets' "Twin Towers" in the 1980s.

8. True or false? Mario Andretti, John Elway, and Jose Canseco have twin siblings.

9. Which two Michigan State basketball coaches have won NCAA titles?

10. If all major league players, past and present, were lined up alphabetically, who would be first in line?

ANSWERS

1. Paul and Lloyd Waner
2. Shaquille O'Neal
3. Jacques Plante
4. The right eye
5. Steve Cauthen
6. The New York Giants, 15-13, over the 49ers — The Giants scored five field goals.
7. Ralph Sampson and Hakeem Olajuwon
8. True
9. Jud Heathcote, 1979 and Tom Izzo, 2000
10. Hank Aaron, right in front of brother, Tommy

Sec. 07

Row 19

Seat 12

Enter
Gate C
Upper Tier

"I know I'm getting better at golf because I'm hitting fewer spectators."

-Former U.S. President Gerald Ford

FULL SEASON TICKET

FORMERLY KNOWN AS

Match the team with its former name.

1.	New York Jets	A.	Seattle Pilots
2.	Sacramento Kings	B.	Winnipeg Jets
3.	New Jersey Devils	C.	Dallas Chaparrals
4.	Baltimore Ravens	D.	Decatur Staleys
5.	San Antonio Spurs	E.	New York Titans
6.	Texas Rangers	F.	Houston Oilers
7.	Phoenix Coyotes	G.	Washington Senators
8.	Chicago Bears	H.	Cincinnati Royals
9.	Milwaukee Brewers	I.	Colorado Rockies
10.	Tennessee Titans	J.	Cleveland Browns

Sec. **82** Row **E** Seat **17**

Enter Gate B

"They measured me when I was sitting down."

*–7'7" basketball center Manute Bol, explaining
why his passport listed him at 5'2"*

ANSWERS

1. E
2. H
3. I
4. J
5. C
6. G
7. B
8. D
9. A
10. F

"Our consistency has been up and down all season."

–Boston Celtics center Robert Parish

Sec. 16

Row 51

Seat 7a

**Enter
Gate G**
Lower Tier

HARDBALL TRIVIA

1. The first player named Rookie of the Year and MVP in the same season was   a) Fernando Valenzuela b) Fred Lynn c) Vida Blue d) Paul Blair

2. The pitcher with the highest ERA of any 300-game winner is a) Early Wynn b) Pud Galvin c) Don Sutton d) Steve Carlton

3. The only Cy Young Award winner from the San Francisco Giants was   a) Bill Swift b) Juan Marichal c) Mike McCormick d) Gaylord Perry

4. Which one doesn't belong, and why? a) Don Mattingly b) Ken Griffey, Jr. c) Dale Long d) Derek Jeter

5. The only player to steal more than 100 bases three years in a row is   a) Rickey Henderson b) Vince Coleman c) Lou Brock d) Mr. Spock

6. The first Japanese pitcher in major league history was a) Hideo Nomo b) Hideki Irabu c) Masanori Murakami d) Chan Ho Park

7. The first pitcher to win the Cy Young Award with less than twenty wins was   a) Tom Seaver b) Greg Maddux c) Roger Clemens d) Tom Glavine

8. The Angel traded to the Mets for Nolan Ryan was a) Dick Schofield b) Jim Fregosi c) Bobby Grich d) Bobby Knoop

9. The record for RBIs in a season is 190, set by a) George Foster b) Lou Gehrig c) Hack Wilson d) Mark McGwire

10. The outfielder with a record eight seasons of forty or more home runs is   a) Ralph Kiner b) Hank Aaron c) Ted Williams d) Albert Belle

ANSWERS

1. B — The Red Sox rookie did it in 1975.

2. A — Wynn had a 3.54 ERA to go with his 300 wins.

3. C — McCormick won it in 1967.

4. D — The others made history by hitting home runs in at least eight consecutive games. He hasn't.

5. B — Coleman stole 110 in 1985, 107 in '86 and 109 in '87 for the St. Louis Cardinals.

6. C — Murakami pitched for the San Francisco Giants in 1964 and '65.

7. A — Seaver's record was 19-10 in 1973.

8. B

9. C — Wilson's record-setting year was 1930.

10. B

FULL SEASON

Sec. 17
Row K
Seat 22
Gate F

"Our players don't do dances in the end zone. We like them to act like they've been there before."

–Lou Holtz

GRAB BAG

1. Who was the first major-leaguer to have his uniform number retired?

2. What was the original name of tennis' U.S. Open?

3. Name the only boxer to fight both Rocky Marciano and Muhammad Ali.

4. Who holds the record for career rushing touchdowns?

5. True or false? Nike is the Greek goddess of victory.

6. Two college basketball players led the nation in scoring three straight years. One was Oscar Robertson. Who was the other?

7. Name the last player from West Point to win the Heisman Trophy.

8. Quick! Who is baseball's all-time stolen base leader?

9. With what ABA team did Julius Erving begin his pro career?

10. Name the first player in the NHL to score all five of his team's goals in a regular season game.

"Exactly how intricate a sport is jogging? You were two years old; you ran after the cat; you pretty much had it mastered."

–Rick Reilly

Sec. 16

Row 51

Seat 7a

Enter Gate G
Lower Tier

ANSWERS

1. Lou Gehrig
2. The U.S. Lawn Tennis Championship
3. Archie Moore
4. Walter Payton, 110 touchdowns
5. True
6. Pete Maravich, 1968-70
7. Pete Dawkins, 1958
8. Rickey Henderson
9. The Virginia Squires
10. Sergei Fedorov, Detroit Red Wings

Sec. 07
Row 19
Seat 12
Enter
Gate C
Upper Tier

"I am the greatest golfer in the world. I just haven't played yet."

–Muhammad Ali

FULL SEASON TICKET

THE NAME GAME

Listed below are the original names of sports figures.
Can you identify them?

1. Walker Smith Jr.
2. Sanford Braun
3. Denton True Young
4. Bobby Moore
5. Lew Alcindor
6. Cornelius McGillicuddy
7. Herman Reese
8. Earvin Johnson
9. Cassius Marcellus Clay
10. Jacques Wilkins

Sec.	Row	Seat	Enter Gate B
82	E	17	

"Skiing is the only sport where you can
spend an arm and a leg to break an arm
and a leg."

–Henry Beard

ANSWERS

1. Sugar Ray Robinson
2. Sandy Koufax
3. Cy Young
4. Ahmad Rashad
5. Kareem Abdul-Jabbar
6. Connie Mack
7. PeeWee Reese
8. Magic Johnson
9. Muhammad Ali
10. Dominique Wilkins

FULL SEASON

Sec. 17
Row K
Seat 22
Gate F

"A puck is a hard rubber disk that hockey players strike when they can't hit each other."

–Jimmy Cannon

FIRST AND TEN

Can you name ...

1. The first coach to take two NFL teams to the Super Bowl?
2. The opponents in the first *Monday Night Football* game?
3. The first NFL team to have two 1,000-yard rushers in one season?
4. The first Heisman Trophy winner?
5. The first NFL team to have a domed stadium as its home field?
6. The winning team in the first college football game?
7. The first team to win four Super Bowls?
8. The first NFL team to have an emblem on its helmets?
9. The first champion of the American Football League?
10. The first player to lead the NFL in rushing in his first three seasons?

ANSWERS

1. Don Shula led the Baltimore Colts and Miami Dolphins to Super Bowls.

2. Cleveland beat the New York Jets, 31-21, in 1970.

3. Larry Csonka had 1,117 yards and Mercury Morris 1,000 yards for the 1972 Miami Dolphins.

4. Jay Berwanger, 1935

5. The Houston Oilers moved into the Astrodome in 1968.

6. Rutgers beat Princeton, 6-4, in 1869. A touchdown, at the time, was worth two points.

7. The Pittsburgh Steelers

8. The 1948 Los Angeles Rams

9. The Houston Oilers defeated the Los Angeles Chargers, 24-16, in the 1960 championship game.

10. Earl Campbell, Houston, 1978-80

Sec. 82   Row E   Seat 17
Enter Gate B

"Pete Sampras does have a weakness. He can't cook."

–Fellow tennis player Michael Chang

MY OLD SCHOOL

Match the NBA player with the college he attended.

1.	Reggie Miller	A. Wake Forest
2.	Latrell Sprewell	B. Duke
3.	Shaquille O'Neal	C. California
4.	Allen Iverson	D. LSU
5.	Grant Hill	E. North Carolina
6.	Antoine Walker	F. Georgetown
7.	Tim Duncan	G. Georgia Tech
8.	Vince Carter	H. Alabama
9.	Stephon Marbury	I. UCLA
10.	Shareef Abdur-Rahim	J. Kentucky

Sec. 16

Row 51

Seat 7a

"I guess we shouldn't be patting them on the bottom anymore."

–Michael Jordan, on relationship with NBA referees due to the addition of female officials

**Enter
Gate G**

Lower Tier

ANSWERS

1. I
2. H
3. D
4. F
5. B
6. J
7. A
8. E
9. G
10. C

"Let me give you an idea how much money that is. By the time he gets a sign from his brain to scratch his groin, he's made $1,600."

-Jay Leno, on Ken Griffey Jr's multi-million dollar contract

| **Sec. 16** |
| **Row 51** |
| **Seat 7a** |
| **Enter Gate G** Lower Tier |

THE TROPHY CASE

Identify the hardware that pertain to this quiz.

1. We'll start easy. The best college football player in America is awarded this trophy.

2. Your team has just won the NHL Championship. What trophy do you carry around on the ice?

3. The NBA Coach of the Year receives what trophy?

4. What's the name of the trophy given to the winning team in the Super Bowl?

5. You've been voted the NHL playoff MVP. What trophy do you get?

6. Name the trophy given to the champion of the Canadian Football League.

7. Every other year, American golfers compete with their European counterparts for this prize. Name it.

8. Your good sportsmanship has won over your NHL peers. What trophy are you awarded?

9. You've just won the James Naismith Award. What did you do to deserve it?

10. Give yourself a trophy if you can name the trophy given to the MVP of the NBA.

ANSWERS

1. The Heisman Trophy
2. The Stanley Cup
3. The Red Auerbach Trophy
4. The Vince Lombardi Trophy
5. The Conn Smythe Trophy
6. The Grey Cup
7. The Ryder Cup
8. The Lady Byng Trophy
9. You were named the best male college basketball player in the country.
10. You're the MVP if you said the Maurice Podoloff Trophy.

FULL SEASON
Sec. 17
Row K
Seat 22
Gate F

"I've just played World War II golf —
out in 39 and back in 45."

–*Lee Trevino*

TENNIS, ANYONE?

How well can you return these serves?

1. What events make up the tennis Grand Slam?

2. Mrs. Hingis was so impressed with this tennis player, she named her daughter after her. Who was she?

3. In 1972, this tennis great was the first woman to be named Athlete of the Year by *Sports Illustrated*. Name her.

4. What year did Rod Laver win his second Grand Slam?

5. Venus and Serena Williams learned their games on the hard courts of what California town?

6. Name the first unseeded player to win the title at Wimbledon.

7. What is the length of a tennis court?

8. As an unseeded seventeen-year-old, who won the 1989 French Open over Stefan Edberg?

9. In 1979, she became the youngest U.S. Open women's champion at the age of 16 years, 8 months, 28 days. Do you know her?

10. In the 1990s, he won twelve majors, including six Wimbledon titles. Who is he?

ANSWERS

1. The Australian Open, French Open, Wimbledon and U.S. Open

2. Martina was named after Martina Navratilova.

3. Billie Jean King

4. 1969

5. Compton, CA

6. Boris Becker

7. The court is 78 feet long.

8. Michael Chang

9. Tracy Austin

10. Pete Sampras

"Why doesn't the fattest man in the world become a hockey goalie?"

-Wright Stevens

Sec. 16

Row 51

Seat 7a

Enter Gate G

Lower Tier

FOUR-LETTER WORDS

The answers are last names with four letters.

1. He was the second baseman in Abbott and Costello's "Who's on First" routine.

2. He's the only tennis player to win four straight titles at the French Open.

3. He's second to Wayne Gretzky as the NHL's all-time regular season scoring leader.

4. He won the most batting titles in major league history.

5. He was the first number one draft pick in the history of the NBA's Charlotte Hornets.

6. He was the youngest major-leaguer to hit fifty home runs in a season.

7. He's the NFL record-holder for most interceptions in a season.

8. He had the longest career in baseball history with twenty-seven years of service.

9. He's the pride of French Lick, Indiana.

10. He pitched for the Red Sox and Yankees, compiling a 94-46 won-loss record and a 2.28 lifetime ERA.

ANSWERS

1. What
2. Bjorn Borg
3. Gordie Howe with 2,358 points
4. Ty Cobb won twelve batting crowns.
5. J.R. Reid
6. Willie Mays hit 51 home runs at the age of 24.
7. Dick "Night Train" Lane had 14 INTs in 1952.
8. Nolan Ryan
9. Larry Bird
10. Babe Ruth

Sec. 07

Row 19

Seat 12

Enter
Gate C
Upper Tier

**"Sure the fight was fixed.
I fixed it with my right hand."**

–George Foreman

FULL SEASON TICKET

GRAB BAG

1. Who finished the 1968 Masters tied for first, but inadvertantly signed an incorrect scorecard and was disqualified?

2. Quick! What was Wayne Gretzky's uniform number?

3. What football coach had the misfortune to follow Vince Lombardi in Green Bay?

4. Did Cy Young ever win the Cy Young Award?

5. Name the NHL legend nicknamed "The Rocket."

6. What year did speed-skater Eric Heiden win five Olympic gold medals?

7. What lineman played in the most consecutive games in the history of the NFL?

8. Name the first filly to win the Kentucky Derby.

9. How wide is home plate in baseball?

10. Name the last college basketball team to have a perfect season. Who was its coach?

ANSWERS

1. Roberto DeVincenzo

2. It was number 99.

3. Phil Bengston lasted three years, leaving after the 1970 season with a record of 20-21-1.

4. No

5. Montreal's Maurice Richard

6. 1980

7. Defensive end Jim Marshall of the Minnesota Vikings

8. Favored Regret, 1915

9. Home plate is seventeen inches wide.

10. The 1976 Indiana University team, coached by Bobby Knight

---

"No, I clean giraffe ears."

–Former NBA forward Elvin Hayes,
when asked if he played basketball

Sec. 16

Row 51

Seat 7a

**Enter
Gate G**
Lower Tier

HALLOWED HALLS

Match the Hall of Fame with its location.

1. Bowling		A. Cooperstown, NY
2. Swimming		B. Detroit, MI
3. Tennis		C. Canton, OH
4. Boxing		D. Toronto, Canada
5. Basketball		E. Canastota, NY
6. Hockey		F. Pinehurst, NC
7. Golf		G. Ft. Lauderdale, FL
8. Football		H. Springfield, MA
9. Baseball		I. St. Louis, MO
10. Polish American Sports HOF		J. Newport, RI

Sec. **82**   Row **E**   Seat **17**

Enter Gate B

"Nobody goes to that restaurant anymore. It's too crowded."

–Yogi Berra

ANSWERS

1. I
2. G
3. J
4. E
5. H
6. D
7. F
8. C
9. A
10. B

	Sec. 16
"They broke it to me gently. The manager came up to me before a game and told me they didn't allow visitors in the clubhouse." *–Bob Uecker, on being cut by a baseball team*	Row 51
	Seat 7a
	Enter Gate G Lower Tier

YOU WERE THERE

On January 12, 1969 the New York Jets upset the
heavily-favored Baltimore Colts, 16-7, to win Super Bowl III.
How much do you know about the game?

1. Where was the game played?

2. Who was named the game's MVP?

3. Name the opposing head coaches.

4. Who scored the winning team's only touchdown?

5. Which Colt starting quarterback earned the regular-season
   MVP Award, filling in for the injured Johnny Unitas?

6. Who was the Colts' halfback who rushed for 116 yards in
   a losing cause?

7. One of the Colts' starting defensive ends was the number-one
   pick in the first combined AFL-NFL draft in 1967. Who
   was he?

8. Name the Jets placekicker who accounted for the rest of the
   team's points with three field goals.

9. Who was the only Baltimore player to cross the goal line for
   a touchdown?

10. Future Hall of Fame receiver Don Maynard was stopped
    without a catch. But the Jets other split end caught eight
    passes for 133 yards. Name him.

ANSWERS

1. The game was played in the Orange Bowl in Miami.

2. Quarterback Joe Namath was the game's MVP.

3. Weeb Ewbank coached the Jets, while the Colts were led by Don Shula.

4. Fullback Matt Snell

5. Earl Morrall

6. Tom Matte

7. Bubba Smith was drafted out of Michigan State.

8. Jim Turner

9. Fullback Jerry Hill

10. George Sauer Jr.

Sec. 07

Row 19

Seat 12

Enter
Gate C
Upper Tier

FULL SEASON TICKET

"I want to be the fastest woman in the world — in a manner of speaking."

–Auto racer Shirley Muldowney

KEEPING IT SIMPLE

The following questions can be answered
with a simple "yes" or "no."

1. Did Mickey Mantle ever hit four home runs in a game?

2. Can a racehorse's name be longer than eighteen letters?

3. Was miniature golf originally called "Tom Thumb Golf"?

4. Is the score of a forfeited baseball game 9-0?

5. Was Michael Jordan ever cut from his high school basketball team?

6. Was Hank Aaron the first major-leaguer to hit 500 home runs and get 3,000 hits?

7. Did golfer Lee Trevino ever win The Masters?

8. Did Grant Hill share NBA Rookie of the Year honors with Jason Kidd?

9. Was Joe Namath ever named an All-American quarterback at Alabama?

10. Did Nolan Ryan ever win a Cy Young Award?

ANSWERS

1. No
2. No
3. Yes
4. Yes
5. Yes
6. Yes
7. No
8. Yes
9. No
10. No

"Statistics are used by baseball fans in much the same way that a drunk leans against a street lamp; it's there more for support than enlightenment."

–Announcer Vin Scully

| Sec. 16 |
| Row 51 |
| Seat 7a |
| Enter Gate G
Lower Tier |

ONLY TEAMS

Which was …

1. The only NFL team owned by a city?

2. The only college basketball team not located in any of the fifty states to win the NCAA Championship?

3. The only NHL team to go unbeaten in thirty-five straight games?

4. The only NBA expansion team to qualify for the playoffs in its first season?

5. The only team to be held without a touchdown in the Super Bowl?

6. The only college basketball team to win NCAA and NIT titles in the same year?

7. The only team in professional sports with an insect's name?

8. The only NFL team with an emblem on just one side of its helmet?

9. The only team to win sixteen NBA titles?

10. The only team to have a father-son combination hit home runs in the same inning of the same game?

ANSWERS

1. The Green Bay Packers

2. Georgetown University which is located in Washington, DC

3. The Philadelphia Flyers did it in 1980.

4. The Chicago Bulls made the playoffs after the 1966-67 season.

5. Miami lost, 24-3, in Super Bowl VI.

6. The City College of New York was the dual champ in 1950.

7. The Charlotte Hornets

8. The Pittsburgh Steelers

9. The Boston Celtics

10. Ken Griffey Sr. and Jr. both homered for the Seattle Mariners in 1990.

FULL SEASON

Sec. 17
Row K
Seat 22
Gate F

"I'm playing like Tarzan — and scoring like Jane."

-Golfer Chi Chi Rodriguez

FIRST BASE

Can you name ...

1. The first major-leaguer to hit four consecutive homers in a game?

2. The Cubs' opponent in the first night game at Wrigley Field?

3. The first major league team to wear numbers on the backs of their uniforms?

4. The first catcher to hit thirty or more home runs in his rookie season?

5. The player who hit the first grand slam in major league All-Star history?

6. The first player to win the Cy Young Award and Rookie of the Year Award in the same year?

7. The first player to hit forty or more home runs and steal forty or more bases in the same season?

8. The teams in Major League Baseball's first night game?

9. The first Little Leaguer to make it to the majors?

10. The first Cub to win the MVP Award while playing for a last-place team?

ANSWERS

1. Lou Gehrig, 1932

2. The Philadelphia Phillies

3. The 1929 New York Yankees

4. The Dodgers' Mike Piazza, 1993

5. Fred Lynn, Boston Red Sox, 1988

6. Fernando Valenzuela, Los Angeles Dodgers, 1981

7. Oakland's Jose Canseco hit 42 home runs and stole 40 bases in 1988.

8. The Reds beat the Phillies, 2-1, in 1935.

9. Joey Jay made his debut with the Milwaukee Braves in 1953.

10. Andre Dawson, 1987

Sec. 82 Row E Seat 17 Enter Gate B

"I went to bed and I was old and washed up.
I woke up a rookie. What could be better?"

*–Golfer Ray Floyd, when he turned 50 and
qualified for the Senior Tour*

DUFFER'S DELIGHT

See if you can stay in the fairway with these questions.

1. What were the only two majors Bobby Jones didn't win in his career?

2. What's the maximum number of clubs you're allowed to carry in your bag during a match?

3. What is Fuzzy Zoeller's real name?

4. Name the only major won by Johnny Miller.

5. 1988 was the first year a player earned a million dollars on the PGA Tour. Who was he?

6. Quick! In what month is The Masters played?

7. What year was the first U.S. Open played?

8. Who holds the PGA Tour record for career wins?

9. What pro golfer is nicknamed "The Walrus"?

10. Name the only major not won by Arnold Palmer.

ANSWERS

1. Jones never won the PGA Championship or The Masters.

2. Fourteen

3. Frank Urban Zoeller

4. Miller took the 1970 U.S. Open title.

5. Curtis Strange

6. The Masters takes place on the second weekend of April every year.

7. 1895

8. Sam Snead had a career-high 84 wins.

9. Craig Stadler

10. Palmer never won a PGA Championship in his career.

"Me — on instant replay."

–Derek Sanderson, when asked to name the best hockey player he ever saw

Sec. 16
Row 51
Seat 7a
Enter Gate G Lower Tier

HIGH FIVE

1. He led the NBA in field goal percentage five straight seasons. Name him.

2. Five U.S. cities have had teams win a Super Bowl and the Stanley Cup. How many can you name?

3. True or false? No driver has won the Indianapolis 500 five times.

4. Who was the first athlete to win five gold medals in a Winter Olympics?

5. Name the five events in the modern pentathlon.

6. The Dallas Cowboys have had five coaches in their history. Name them.

7. Five amateur golfers have won the U.S. Open. Francis Ouimet, Jerry Travers, Chick Evans and John Goodman are four of them. Who is number five?

8. There are five major-leaguers with more than 3,000 career hits who have never won a batting title. How many do you know?

9. The Flyers and Penguins battled for five overtimes in a 2000 NHL playoff game, the longest in 64 years. Who won the game?

10. What three major-leaguers homered twenty or more times in a year for five different teams?

ANSWERS

1. Wilt Chamberlain, 1964-69

2. Pittsburgh (Steelers and Penguins), Chicago (Bears and Blackhawks), New York (Jets, Giants, Islanders and Rangers), Denver (Broncos and Colorado Avalanche), Dallas (Cowboys and North Stars)

3. True

4. Speed-skater Eric Heiden accomplished the feat in 1980 at Lake Placid, NY.

5. Riding, fencing, shooting, swimming and running

6. Tom Landry, Jimmy Johnson, Barry Switzer, Chan Gailey and Dave Campo

7. Bobby Jones

8. Eddie Collins, Dave Winfield, Lou Brock, Robin Yount and Cal Ripken Jr.

9. The Flyers, 2-1

10. Dave Winfield did it with the Padres, Yankees, Angels, Blue Jays, and Twins. Bobby Bonds was the player for the Giants, Yankees, Angels, Rangers and Indians. Jack Clark was the batter for the Giants, Cardinals, Yankees, Padres and Red Sox.

GRAB BAG

1. What is the name of the emblem on the New Orleans Saints helmet?

2. Who has the most career World Series home runs?

3. Who won the 2000 Indianapolis 500?

4. What boxer did Sonny Liston beat to become heavyweight champ of the world?

5. What NHL player receives the Vezina Trophy?

6. Who were the first three pitchers elected to the Baseball Hall of Fame?

7. Name the starting quarterbacks in the first Super Bowl.

8. What three events comprise horse racing's Triple Crown?

9. What animal is the mascot for the football team at the U.S. Naval Academy?

10. Who was the first baseball player featured on a U.S. postage stamp?

ANSWERS

1. It's called a *fleur de lis*.

2. Mickey Mantle hit eighteen World Series home runs.

3. Juan Montoya

4. Floyd Patterson

5. The season's best goaltender receives the award.

6. Christy Mathewson, Walter Johnson and Cy Young

7. Bart Starr started for Green Bay, while Len Dawson had the honors for the Chiefs.

8. The Kentucky Derby, Preakness and Belmont Stakes

9. The Middies' mascot is a goat.

10. Jackie Robinson, 1982

Sec.	Row	Seat		
82	E	17	Enter Gate B	"I don't think the coach likes me. He told me to stand in front of the Zamboni." *–Snoopy*

HOME COURT ADVANTAGE

Match the NBA team with the arena it calls "home."

1. Celtics
2. Pistons
3. Rockets
4. 76ers
5. Cavaliers
6. Timberwolves
7. Jazz
8. Mavericks
9. Trail Blazers
10. Pacers

A. The Palace of Auburn Hills
B. Gund Arena
C. Target Center
D. The Rose Garden
E. Conseco Fieldhouse
F. First Union Center
G. Reunion Arena
H. Delta Center
I. Fleet Center
J. The Summit

Sec. 07

Row 19

Seat 12

Enter
Gate C

Upper Tier

"It's like a menu: they can look, but they can't afford it."

-Tennis' glamour girl Anna Kournikova, about her male fans

FULL SEASON TICKET

ANSWERS

1. I
2. A
3. J
4. F
5. B
6. C
7. H
8. G
9. D
10. E

FULL SEASON

Sec. 17
Row K
Seat 22
Gate F

"I don't know — I only played there nine years."

–Former Dallas Cowboy Walt Garrison,
when asked if coach Tom Landry ever smiled

DEPARTMENT OF WEIGHTS AND MEASURES

Do you know …

1. The length of a bowling lane?

2. The height of a tennis net directly in the center?

3. The width of a soccer goal, in feet?

4. How long a furlong is in horse racing?

5. The distance from home plate to second base on a big league field?

6. The height from the floor to a basketball rim?

7. How deep home plate in baseball is, front to back?

8. The distance from the ground to the uprights in football?

9. The length and width of an NHL rink?

10. The minimum depth of a golf hole?

ANSWERS

1. 60 feet
2. 3 feet
3. 24 feet
4. 1/8 of a mile
5. 127 feet, 3 3/8 inches
6. 10 feet
7. 17 inches
8. 10 feet
9. 200 feet X 85 feet
10. 4 inches

"They talk about the economy this year. Hey, my hairline is in recession, my waistline is in inflation. All together, I'm in a depression." *-University of Utah basketball coach Rick Majerus*	**Sec. 16** **Row 51** **Seat 7a** **Enter Gate G** Lower Tier

YOU WERE THERE

On March 26, 1979 Magic Johnson led Michigan State to its first NCAA basketball title, beating Indiana State and Larry Bird, 75-64. How much do you know about the game?

1. True or false? Indiana State was ranked number one going into the tournament.

2. The Spartans' head coach was in his third year at the helm. Name him.

3. What was the team nickname of Indiana State?

4. Michigan State held Larry Bird to how many points?

5. True or false? Indiana State was the first undefeated team to lose in a championship game.

6. Name the Final Four Most Outstanding Player.

7. Two eventual NBA forwards played in the title game for Michigan State. Who were they?

8. Who was the head coach for Indiana State?

9. True or false? Indiana State is the only school to reach the Final Four in its one and only NCAA Tournament appearance.

10. True or false? The game marked the end of Magic Johnson's college career.

ANSWERS

1. True — They were 33-0.
2. Jud Heathcote
3. The Sycamores
4. Bird was held to nineteen points, making only seven of twenty-one points.
5. False — In 1961, Ohio State lost to Cincinnati.
6. Magic Johnson
7. Greg Kelser and Jay Vincent
8. Bill Hodges
9. True
10. True — Johnson declared hardship and was drafted by the Lakers later that year.

Sec. 07

Row 19

Seat 12

Enter
Gate C
Upper Tier

"We can't win at home. We can't win on the road. As a general manager, I just can't figure out where else to play."

-Orlando Magic GM Pat Williams

FULL SEASON TICKET

BY THE NUMBERS

Do you know ...

1. The number of positions mentioned in Abbott and Costello's "Who's on First" routine?

2. The number of NFL teams with bird nicknames?

3. The number of consecutive tournaments won by golfer Byron Nelson in 1945?

4. The number of teams in the United States Football League in 1982, its inaugural season?

5. The number of career strikeouts by the leading left-handed strikeout artist, Steve Carlton?

6. Walter Payton's uniform number?

7. The number of U.S. Open titles won by tennis great, Bjorn Borg?

8. The number of stitches on an official major league baseball?

9. The number of time-outs, per game, an NFL team is allowed?

10. The number of events in the modern pentathlon?

ANSWERS

1. Eight — Right field was left out.
2. Five (Cardinals, Eagles, Falcons, Ravens and Seahawks)
3. Eleven
4. Twelve
5. 4,136
6. Thirty-four
7. Zero
8. 108
9. Six (three per half)
10. Five

"You know, when the World Cup is over, all these people will go home. Which means the only people bouncing balls off their head will be the Chicago Cubs outfielders."

-Jay Leno

Sec. 16

Row 51

Seat 7a

Enter Gate G

Lower Tier

TRIVIQUATIONS

Test your math and your hoops knowledge.
Fill in the number portion of the answers suggested
by the clues and solve the Trivquation.

1. (Charles Barkley's number + Walt Frazier's number)
   X (halves in a game) =

2. (UCLA's record winning streak)

3. $\dfrac{\text{(seconds in shot clock)}}{\text{(NBA roster size)}}$ + (Kareem's retirement age) =

4. (Jerry West's uniform number)

5. (total of NBA teams) - (the height of the rim) =

6. (number of consecutive seasons Abdul-Jabbar
   scored a thousand or more points)

7. $\dfrac{\text{(Patrick Ewing's number)}}{\text{(Lakers' winning streak)}}$ + $\dfrac{\text{(Atlantic Division teams)}}{\text{(Pacific Division teams)}}$ =

8. (rounds in NBA draft)

9. (shots in technical foul + Knick scoring champs)
   X (Magic's number) =

10. (teams in NCAA tournament)

ANSWERS

1. $(34 + 10) \times 2 =$
2. 88

3. $\dfrac{24}{12} + 42 =$
4. 44

5. $29 - 10 =$
6. 19

7. $\dfrac{33}{33} + \dfrac{7}{7} =$
8. 2

9. $(1 + 1) \times 32 =$
10. 64

Sec.	Row	Seat	
82	E	17	Enter Gate B

"I went through life as a player
to be named later."

-Joe Garagiola

ONLY YOU

Can you name them?

1. He's the only NHL defenseman to win a scoring title.

2. He's the only second baseman in major league history to win back-to-back MVP Awards.

3. He's the only golfer to win the U.S. Open, British Open and Masters in the same year.

4. He's the only quarterback to play in five Super Bowls.

5. He's the only boxer to beat Gene Tunney, winning by decision in a 1922 light-heavyweight bout.

6. He's the only pitcher to hit two home runs while throwing a no-hitter.

7. He's the only player to rush for more than 5,000 yards for each of two NFL teams.

8. He's the only man to win the World Series MVP Award with two different teams.

9. He's the only undefeated heavyweight champion in professional boxing history.

10. He's the only Celtic to have been a teammate of both Bill Russell and Larry Bird.

ANSWERS

1. Bobby Orr won it in 1970 and '75.

2. Joe Morgan was most valuable in both 1975 and '76.

3. Ben Hogan, 1953

4. John Elway, Denver

5. Harry Greb

6. Rick Wise, Philadelphia, 1971

7. Eric Dickerson accomplished it with the Rams and the Colts.

8. Reggie Jackson, with Oakland in 1973 and the Yankees in 1977

9. Rocky Marciano finished at 49-0.

10. Don Chaney

"'Sorry Mickey,' the Lord said, 'but I wanted to give you the word personally. You can't go to heaven because of the way you acted down on earth, but would you mind signing a dozen baseballs?'"

–Mickey Mantle, talking about a recurring nightmare

| Sec. 16 |
| Row 51 |
| Seat 7a |
| Enter Gate G |
| Lower Tier |

INITIALLY SPEAKING

The number on the left is based upon the first letters
for the words on the right.

1. 3 = S. and Y.O.
2. 18 = H. on a G.C.
3. 10 = F. in B.
4. 100 = Y. on a F.F.
5. 3 = P. in a H.G.
6. 48 = M. in a P.B.G.
7. 4 = G. to W. the W.S.
8. .367 = L.B.A. of T.C.
9. 1 = P. for a F.T.
10. 7 = N.-H. by N.R.

FULL SEASON

Sec. 17
Row K
Seat 22
Gate F

"If it wasn't for golf, I'd probably be a caddie today."

–*George Archer*

ANSWERS

1. Strikes and You're Out
2. Holes on a Golf Course
3. Frames in Bowling
4. Yards on a Football Field
5. Periods in a Hockey Game
6. Minutes in a Pro Basketball Game
7. Games to Win the World Series
8. Lifetime Batting Average of Ty Cobb
9. Point for a Free Throw
10. No-Hitters by Nolan Ryan

Sec. 07

Row 19

Seat 12

Enter
Gate C

Upper Tier

**"I went fishing with a dotted line.
I caught every other fish."**

–Comedian Steven Wright

FULL SEASON TICKET

PIGSKIN POTPOURRI

1. Tampa Bay's first NFL win after twenty-six straight losses came against what team?

2. Hall of Famer Lawrence Taylor was the second pick in the 1981 draft. Who was the first?

3. Brothers Joey, Keith, Ross and Jim all played in the NFL. What is their last name?

4. Name the first African-American player to win the Heisman Trophy.

5. This Hall of Famer was the last player to wear a helmet without a face mask. Name him.

6. What two schools play for the Little Brown Jug?

7. Who was the first coach to both win and lose a Super Bowl game?

8. Name the Jones who was one of the Rams' "Fearsome Foursome."

9. Who was the legendary Grambling coach with more than 400 career wins?

10. Quick! How many games does a team play in the NFL regular season?

ANSWERS

1. New Orleans, in 1977
2. Heisman Trophy winner George Rogers was taken by the Saints.
3. Browner
4. Ernie Davis, Syracuse, 1961
5. Receiver Tommy McDonald of the Philadelphia Eagles
6. Michigan and Minnesota
7. Hank Stram
8. David "Deacon" Jones
9. Eddie Robinson
10. Sixteen

"I want to gain fifteen hundred or two thousand yards, whichever comes first."

–Running back George Rogers

Sec. 16
Row 51
Seat 7a
Enter Gate G Lower Tier

GRAB BAG

1. Who were the two players named co-winners of the NBA's 1999-2000 Rookie of the Year Award?

2. This player set a major league record in 1996, when he had nine RBIs, accounting for all of his team's runs. Do you know him?

3. Name the NHL great who had his number 9 retired by two teams.

4. What is the Super Bowl MVP award called?

5. Who is the official baseball manufacturer for Major League Baseball?

6. Quick! Who was the first coach of the Phoenix Suns?

7. Has a left-handed quarterback ever won a Super Bowl?

8. What baseball stadium was the first to have a retractable roof?

9. True or false? Before Mickey Mantle, no Yankees player had ever worn the number 7.

10. This Japanese-owned horse dominated the 2000 Kentucky Derby, but was upset in the Preakness. Name him.

ANSWERS

1. Steve Francis, Rockets and Elton Brand, Bulls
2. Mike Greenwell did it for the Red Sox against Seattle.
3. Bobby Hull, by the Chicago Blackhawks and the then-Winnipeg Jets.
4. It's called the Pete Rozelle Award.
5. The Rawling Sporting Goods Company
6. Johnny Kerr
7. Yes, twice — Steve Young and Ken Stabler
8. Toronto's Skydome
9. False — The number was previously worn by Cliff Mapes.
10. Fusaichi Pegasus

"We were so poor, every Christmas Eve my old man would go outside and shoot his gun, then come in and tell us kids that Santa Claus had committed suicide."

–Boxer Jake LaMotta

Sec. 16

Row 51

Seat 7a

Enter Gate G

Lower Tier

WHO AM I?

1. A former NFL coach, I'm now steering my way through the Winston Cup circuit as a car owner.

2. I became the first player to hit home runs in my first two World Series at-bats in 1972.

3. Elected to the Basketball Hall of Fame in 2000, I won three straight NBA scoring titles in the mid-1970s.

4. As a member of the Cleveland Indians, I became the only player to hit a home run from each side of the plate in the same inning.

5. I am the 1993 Heisman Trophy winner who went on to a career as a point guard in the NBA.

6. The first golfer to win the career Grand Slam, I was also credited with inventing the sand wedge.

7. I'm the only player to win the MVP Award in both the American and National Leagues.

8. Known as "The Big E," I played exactly fifty thousand minutes in my NBA career.

9. In 1995, I became the first congressman to be inducted into the Pro Football Hall of Fame.

10. I was the man who played center at UCLA immediately after Kareem and right before Bill Walton. My teams won three NCAA titles.

ANSWERS

1. Former Washington Redskins coach Joe Gibbs

2. Catcher Gene Tenace of the Oakland A's

3. Bob McAdoo

4. Carlos Baerga did it in 1993.

5. Charlie Ward was a first-round draft pick of the New York Knicks.

6. Gene Sarazen

7. Frank Robinson first won the award with the Reds, then with the Orioles.

8. Former Houston All-American center, Elvin Hayes

9. Former Seattle wide receiver, Steve Largent, who was a U.S. Representative from Oklahoma

10. Steve Patterson

Sec.	Row	Seat	
82	E	17	Enter Gate B

"The similarities between me and my father are different."

–Former big leaguer Dale Berra, the son of that master of malaprops, Yogi

AROUND THE HORN

1. True or false? Tom Seaver won four Cy Young Awards.

2. Name the man who took over as manager of the Yankees after Casey Stengel.

3. Only three shortstops won National League batting titles in the last century, and they all played for the Pittsburgh Pirates in their careers. Can you name them?

4. What two teams were in the first World Series played entirely on artificial turf?

5. Who is the only player to hit two grand slams in the same inning?

6. He's Major League Baseball's leader in career pinch-hits. Name him.

7. Who is the only player to hit fifty home runs in a season more than once, yet retired with fewer than 500 homers?

8. Quick! Name the only two members of the Hall of Fame not affiliated with baseball.

9. Who was the first National League player to win back-to-back MVP Awards?

10. What player had his number 29 retired by both the Twins and the Angels?

ANSWERS

1. False — Seaver won in 1969, '73, and '75.

2. Ralph Houk

3. They were Honus Wagner, Arky Vaughan and Dick Groat.

4. The Phillies and the Royals, 1980

5. Fernando Tatis, St. Louis, 1999

6. Manny Mota had 150 pinch-hits in his career.

7. Ralph Kiner finished his Hall of Fame career with 369 home runs.

8. Comedians Abbott and Costello

9. "Mr. Cub," Ernie Banks, won it in 1958 and '59.

10. Rod Carew

"You give 100 percent in the first half of the game, and if that's not enough, in the second half you give what's left."

–Yogi Berra

| Sec. 16 |
| Row 51 |
| Seat 7a |
| Enter Gate G Lower Tier |

FIRST THINGS FIRST

Can you name ...

1. The player who made the NBA's first three-point shot?

2. The NBA's first African-American head coach?

3. The first player to lead the NBA in scoring and assists in the same season?

4. The first coach of the Portland Trail Blazers?

5. The first guard to win the NBA's Most Valuable Player Award?

6. The coach whose first and only NCAA basketball title came in his last career game in 1977?

7. The first center to lead the NBA in scoring and rebounding?

8. The first woman to play for the Harlem Globetrotters?

9. The first commissioner of the NBA?

10. The first NBA player to get a quadruple double in one game?

ANSWERS

1. Celtics guard Chris Ford sank it in the 1979-80 season, the first year of the rule change.

2. Bill Russell

3. Nate Archibald of the Kansas City Kings did it in the 1972-73 season.

4. Rolland Todd

5. Bob Cousy, Boston, 1956-57

6. Al McGuire, Marquette

7. Neil Johnston, Philadelphia Warriors, 1954-55

8. Lynette Woodard

9. Maurice Podoloff

10. Nate Thurmond had 22 points, 14 rebounds, 13 assists and 12 blocked shots in a 1974 game.

FULL SEASON	Sec. 17 Row K Seat 22 Gate F	"Hello everybody, and welcome to Two Rivers Stadium."
		-San Francisco Giants play-by-play man Hank Greenwald, after he was asked to shorten his pre-game talk at Three Rivers Stadium

MOUNT OLYMPUS

Go for the gold.

1. In 1980, the United States boycotted the Summer Olympics. In what city were they held?

2. This 22-year-old swimmer won four individual gold medals and three relay titles at the 1972 Olympics. Who was he?

3. True or false? The gold medal won by the 1980 U.S. hockey team was this country's first ever in that Olympic sport.

4. Quick! Name the coach of that team.

5. 1968 was the year this athlete won a record fourth consecutive gold medal in the discus throw. Name him.

6. The 1992 Olympics marked the debut of American NBA players. Who was the coach of that Dream Team?

7. What three Olympic events did the great Jesse Owens win in 1936?

8. Name the American runner whose gold medal bid ended when she fell in a tripping incident during the 1984 1,500 meter race.

9. What was the host city when Muhammad Ali, then Cassius Clay, won his 1960 gold medal?

10. Two men have won the decathlon in two straight Olympics. One is Bob Mathias, who won in 1948 and '52. Who is the other?

ANSWERS

1. Moscow

2. Californian Mark Spitz

3. False — The United States had previously won the gold in 1960.

4. Herb Brooks

5. Al Oerter

6. Chuck Daly

7. The 100 meters, 200 meters, and what was known then as the broad jump

8. Mary Decker Slaney

9. Rome

10. Daley Thompson of Great Britain won it in 1980 and '84.

Sec. 07		
Row 19	**"Lots of people look up to Charles Barkley. That's because he's just knocked them down."**	FULL SEASON TICKET
Seat 12		
Enter Gate C	*–Chuck Daly*	
Upper Tier		

SCHOOL DAYS

Match the NFL player with the college he attended.

1.	Tim Couch	A. Southern Mississippi
2.	Edgerrin James	B. Washington
3.	Donovan McNabb	C. Marshall
4.	Terrell Davis	D. Kentucky
5.	Mark Brunell	E. Memphis State
6.	Drew Bledsoe	F. USC
7.	Keyshawn Johnson	G. Miami (FL)
8.	Brett Favre	H. Washington State
9.	Isaac Bruce	I. Georgia
10.	Randy Moss	J. Syracuse

ANSWERS

1. D
2. G
3. J
4. I
5. B
6. H
7. F
8. A
9. E
10. C

Sec. 07

Row 19

Seat 12

Enter
Gate C
Upper Tier

"The reason the (golf) pro tells you to keep your head down is so you can't see him laughing."

–Comedienne Phyllis Diller

FULL SEASON TICKET

HOOP! HOOP! HOORAY!

1. Name the Boston Celtics all-time scoring leader.

2. The Lakers selected Jerry West with the second pick in the 1960 NBA draft. What player was taken ahead of him?

3. Shaquille O'Neal received all but one first place vote in the balloting for the 1999-2000 MVP Award. Who got the other vote?

4. Despite winning nine NBA championships, he was voted Coach of the Year only once. Who was he?

5. Who was the shortest player to win an NBA rebounding title?

6. True or false? Dick Vitale never coached in the NBA.

7. Who was the first player ever chosen in the NBA lottery?

8. What NBA team started out as the Buffalo Braves?

9. Name the only two players to have scored thirty thousand points in their NBA careers.

10. Who is the only player to score fifty or more points in a NBA playoff game five times?

ANSWERS

1. John Havlicek

2. Oscar Robertson

3. Allen Iverson, 76ers

4. Red Auerbach, Boston

5. Charles Barkley was 6 feet, 5 inches tall when he grabbed the crown in 1987.

6. False — Vitale coached the Detroit Pistons in the 1978-79 season, and for 12 games in the 1979-80 season.

7. Patrick Ewing, by the Knicks

8. The Los Angeles Clippers

9. Wilt Chamberlain and Kareem Abdul-Jabbar

10. Michael Jordan, Chicago

FULL SEASON

Sec. 17
Row K
Seat 22
Gate F

"I believe that professional wrestling is real and everything else in the world is fixed."

–Sportswriter Frank Deford

LAST CALL

1. Who was the last manager of baseball's Washington Senators?

2. Name the last man to score six touchdowns in an NFL game.

3. Who was the last National Leaguer to bat .400 in a season?

4. What team was the last stop for pitcher Warren Spahn in his Hall of Fame career?

5. Name the teams that played to the last scoreless tie in the NFL.

6. Who was the last manager of baseball's Brooklyn Dodgers?

7. With what team did football great Johnny Unitas finish his career?

8. Hall of Fame pitcher Robin Roberts began his career with the Phillies. With what team did he end it?

9. What was the last team coached by the legendary Vince Lombardi?

10. Who was the last player to get a hit off pitcher Satchel Paige?

ANSWERS

1. Ted Williams, 1971 — He then moved with the team to Texas for one year, managing the Rangers.

2. In 1965, Gale Sayers struck gold against the 49ers.

3. Bill Terry hit .401 in 1930 for the New York Giants.

4. The San Francisco Giants

5. The Giants and Lions didn't cross the goal line in that game in 1943.

6. Walter Alston — He managed the team in Los Angeles before retiring in 1976.

7. The San Diego Chargers

8. The Chicago Cubs

9. The Washington Redskins

10. Carl Yastrzemski doubled off the then-59-year-old Paige in 1965.

Sec. 07

Row 19

Seat 12

Enter
Gate C
Upper Tier

"I went to a fight the other night and a hockey game broke out."

–Rodney Dangerfield

FULL SEASON TICKET